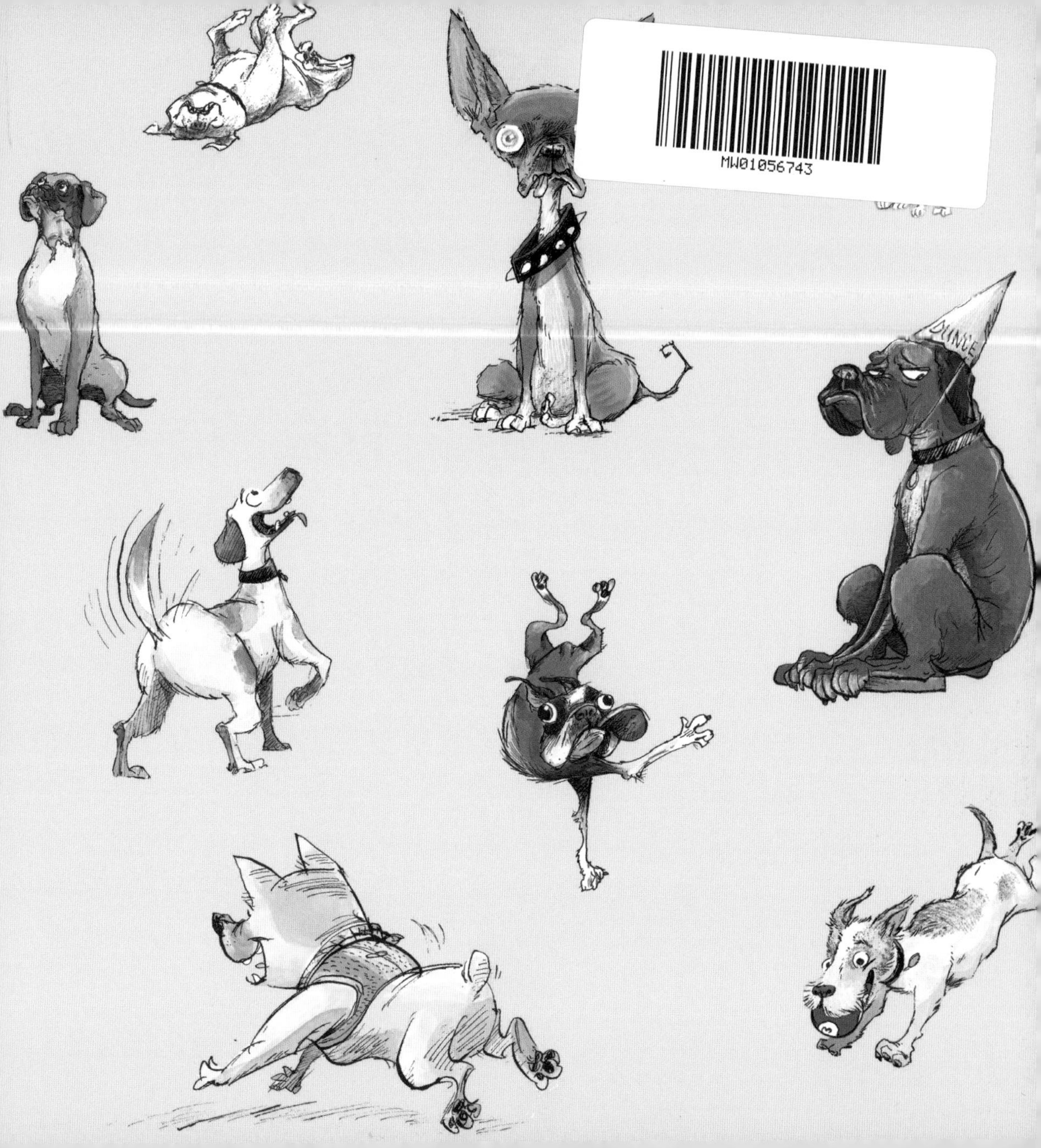
DUNCE

You're not a real™ *dog owner* until...

Scott Dooley & Jason Chatfield

Andrews McMeel
PUBLISHING®

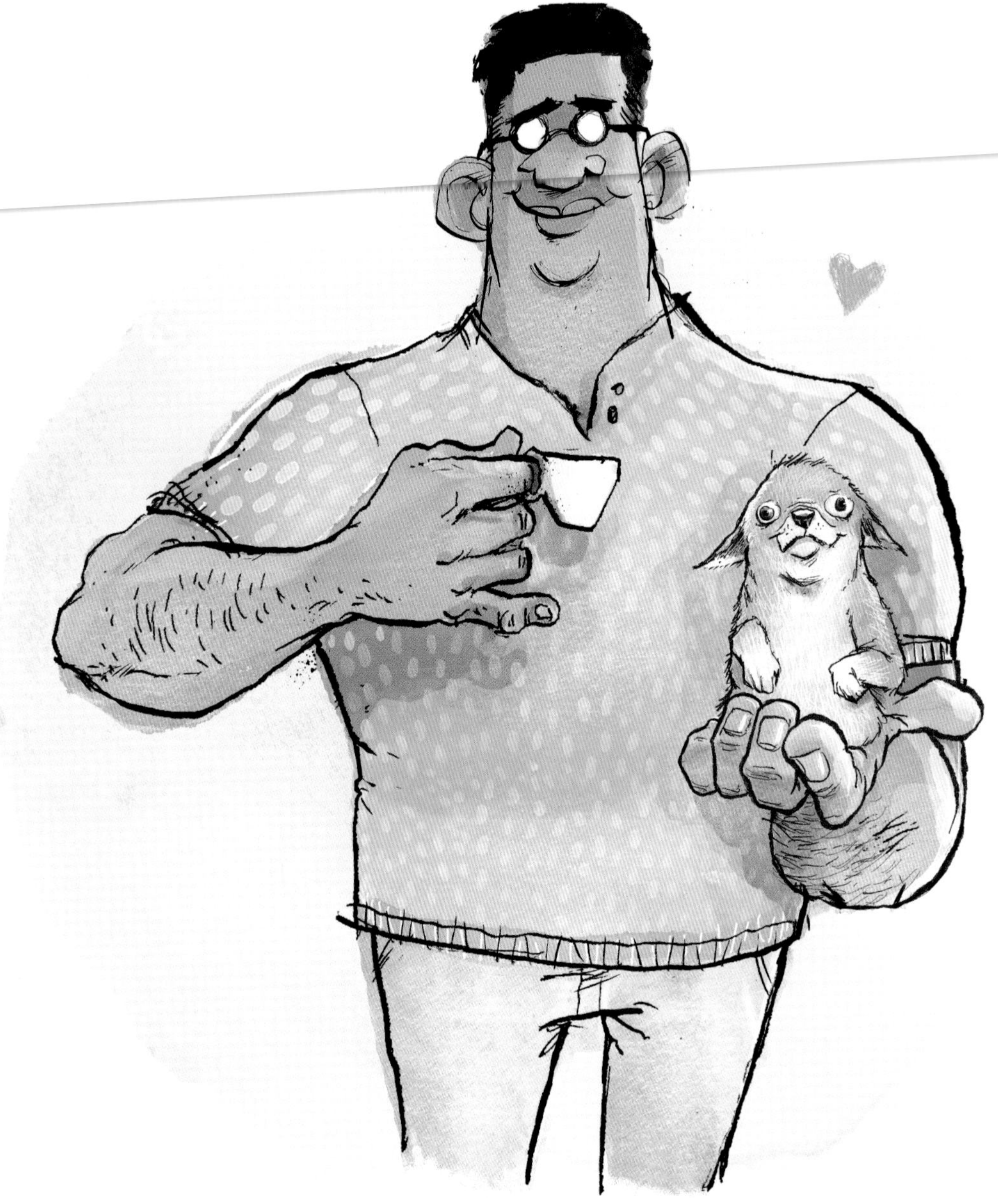

For Morris, Brutus, Walter, Millie, Rusty, Charlie, Ellie, Chloe, Tilly, Poppy, Trixie, and all the other best friends who have brightened our lives and made the world more bearable.

You're not a *real* dog owner until...

...you tell people you've trained your dog not to sleep on the bed.

You're not a *real* dog owner until...

...you set up a "safe zone" for
fireworks and thunder.

You're not a *real* dog owner until...

...you've lost feeling in a leg because you didn't want to wake your dog.

You're not a *real* dog owner until...

...“my puppy did the same thing” is something
you’ve stopped yourself from saying when
someone is talking about their child.

You're not a *real* dog owner until...

...bad behavior is rewarded if it's cute.

You're not a *real* dog owner until...

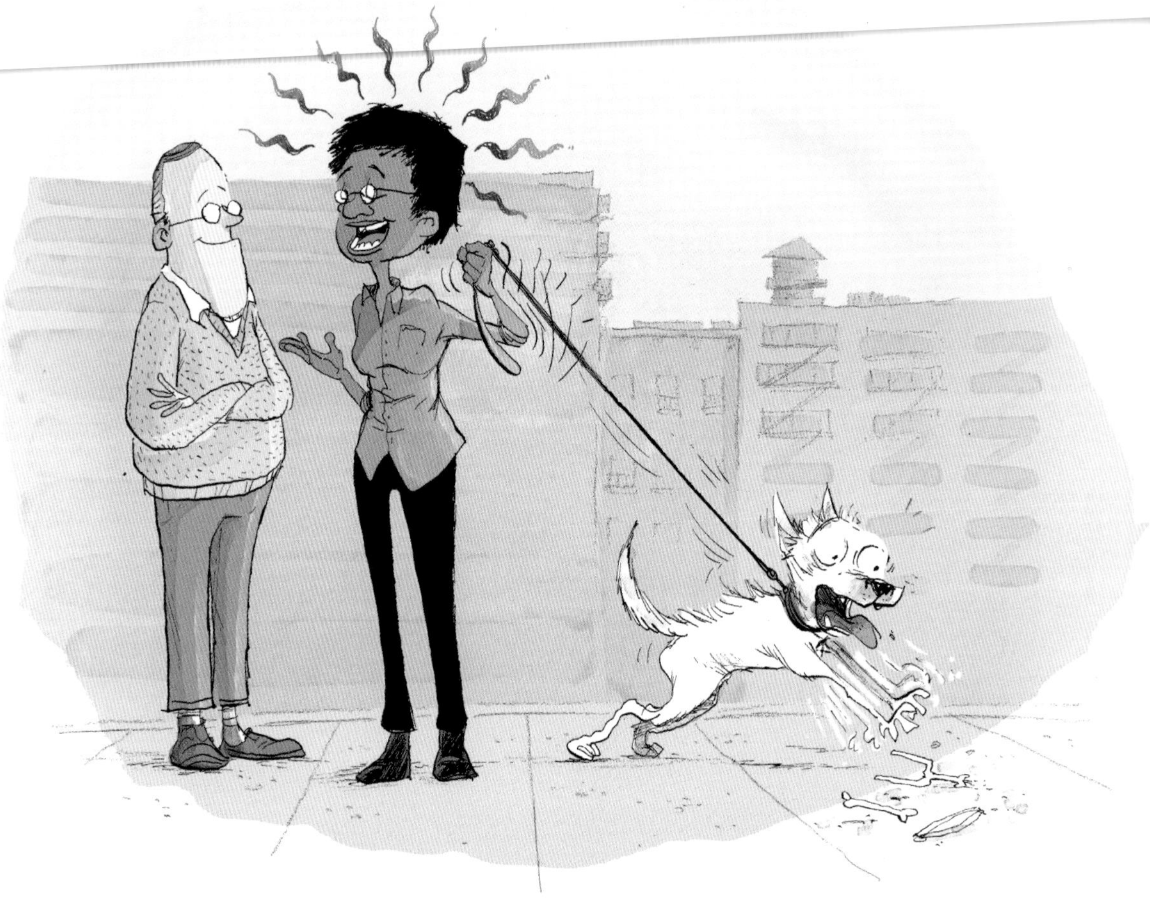

...you develop a sixth sense for chicken bones in your vicinity.

You're not a *real* dog owner until...

...bribery becomes second nature.

You're not a *real* dog owner until...

...only you can say what is and isn't fine
for them to be chewing.

You're not a *real* dog owner until...

...head tilts render you completely helpless.

You're not a *real* dog owner until...

...owners do look like their dogs and you're okay
with that because your dog is the cutest.

You're not a *real* dog owner until...

...your trust issues stem from "guarantees"
on stain removers.

You're not a *real* dog owner until...

...you know something is horribly wrong if you're not greeted the second you enter the house.

You're not a *real* dog owner until...

...the question "What are you eating?"
makes you glad your dog can't talk.

You're not a *real* dog owner until...

...you'd be on a list if you approached people
the way you do dogs.

You're not a *real* dog owner until...

...no matter what you do, you'll never be
as entertaining as an ice cube.

You're not a *real* dog owner until...

...“they'll be tired after this” is a lie
you constantly tell yourself.

You're not a *real* dog owner until...

...you've blamed puppy school results
on the teacher.

You're not a *real* dog owner until...

...holding a treat gives you an insight into
what being a cult leader must be like.

You're not a *real* dog owner until...

...the term "dog whistle" has lost all meaning.

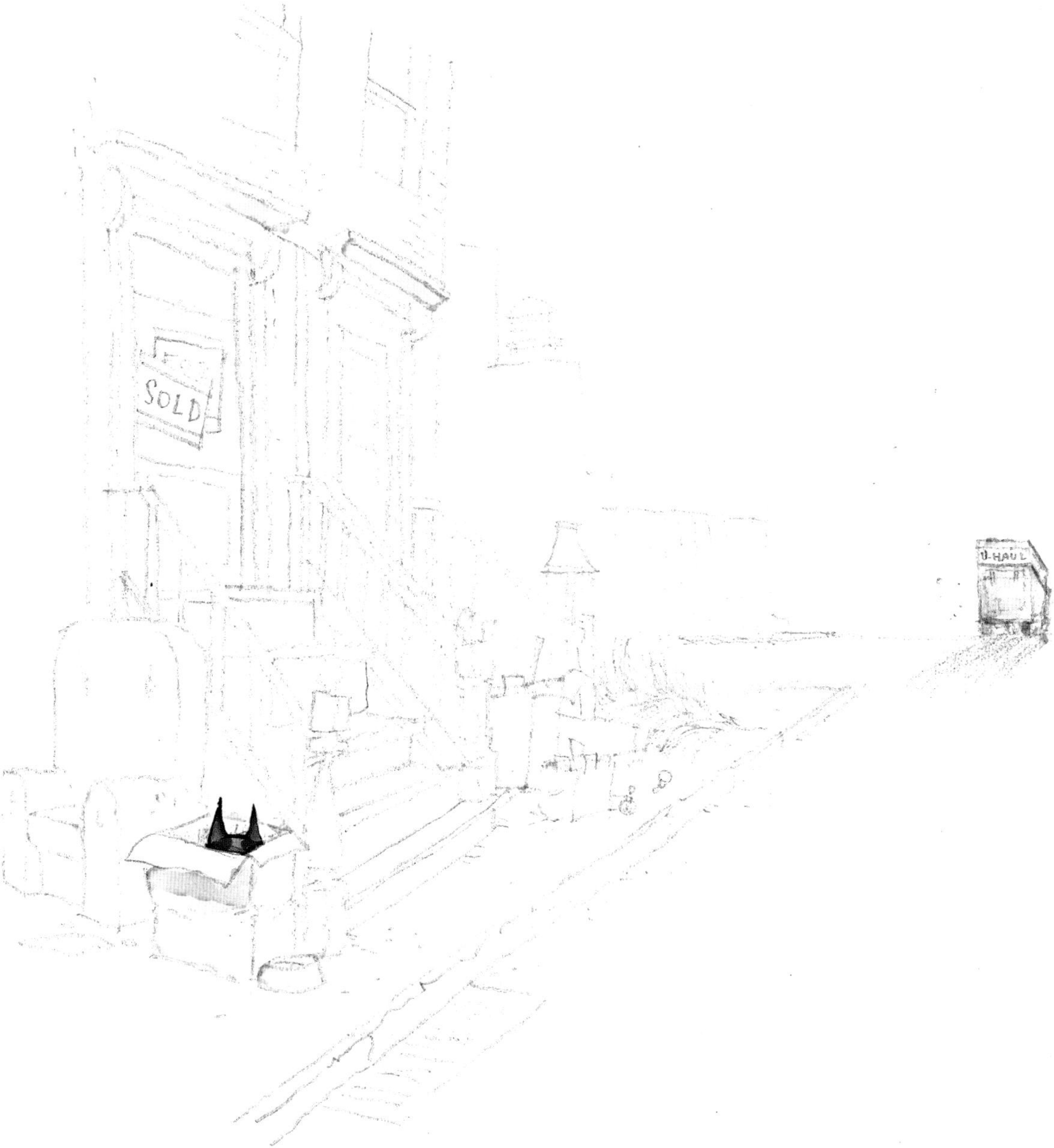
SOLD
U-HAUL

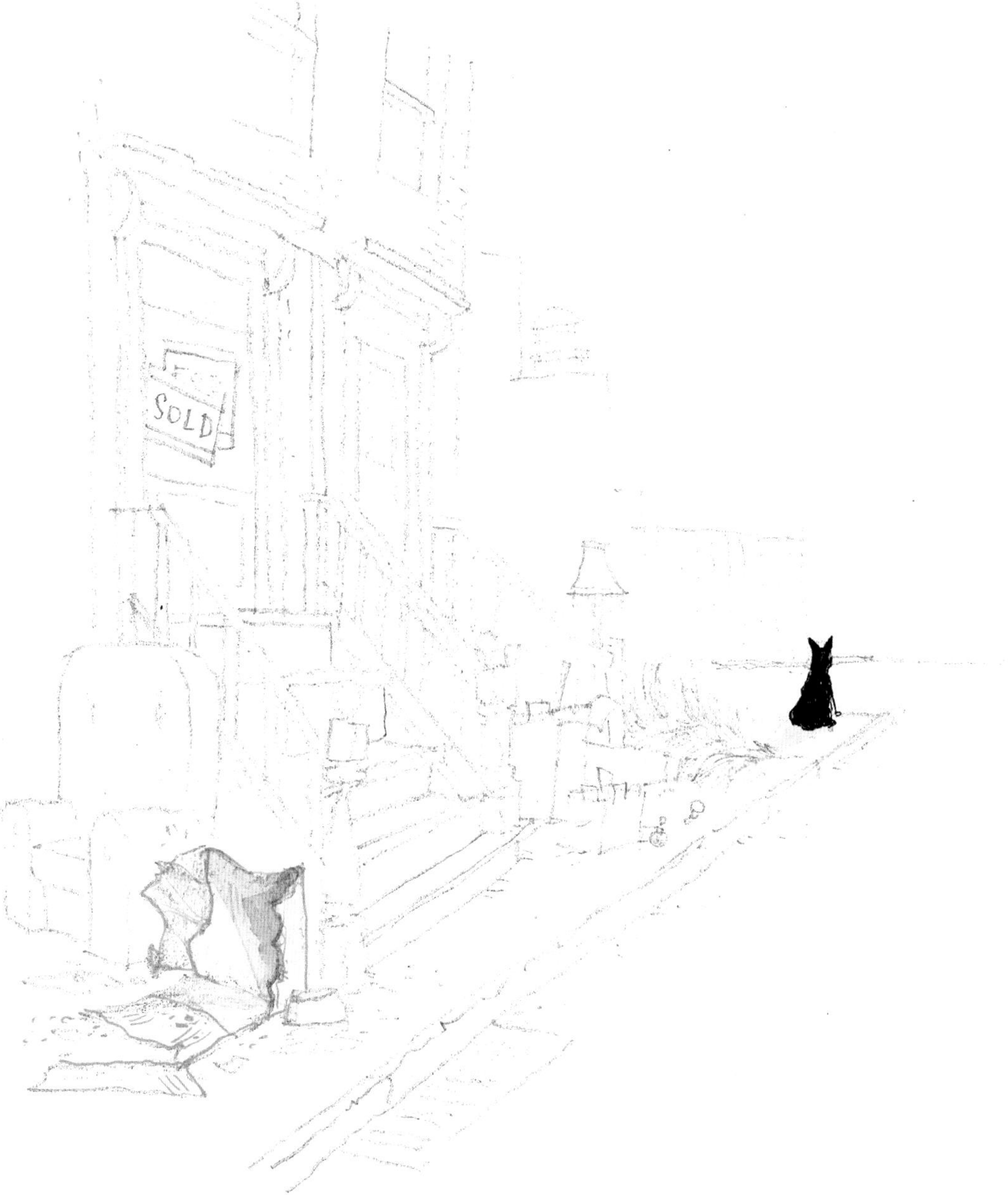
SOLD

You're not a *real* dog owner until...

...messy eaters become VERY easy to identify.

You're not a *real* dog owner until...

...you think you could train the frightening, enormous dog from Harry Potter.

You're not a *real* dog owner until...

...despite all evidence suggesting otherwise,
you're convinced your dog is actually really smart.

You're not a *real* dog owner until...

...documentaries about wolves make you
wonder if you may be spoiling someone.

...you trust your dog's assessment of people more than your own.

You're not a *real* dog owner until...

...you've watched a dog show and wondered
if your dog has what it takes to go "pro."

You're not a *real* dog owner until...

...you honestly believe that the animal
you've seen outwitted by its own tail
would save you in an emergency.

You're not a *real* dog owner until...

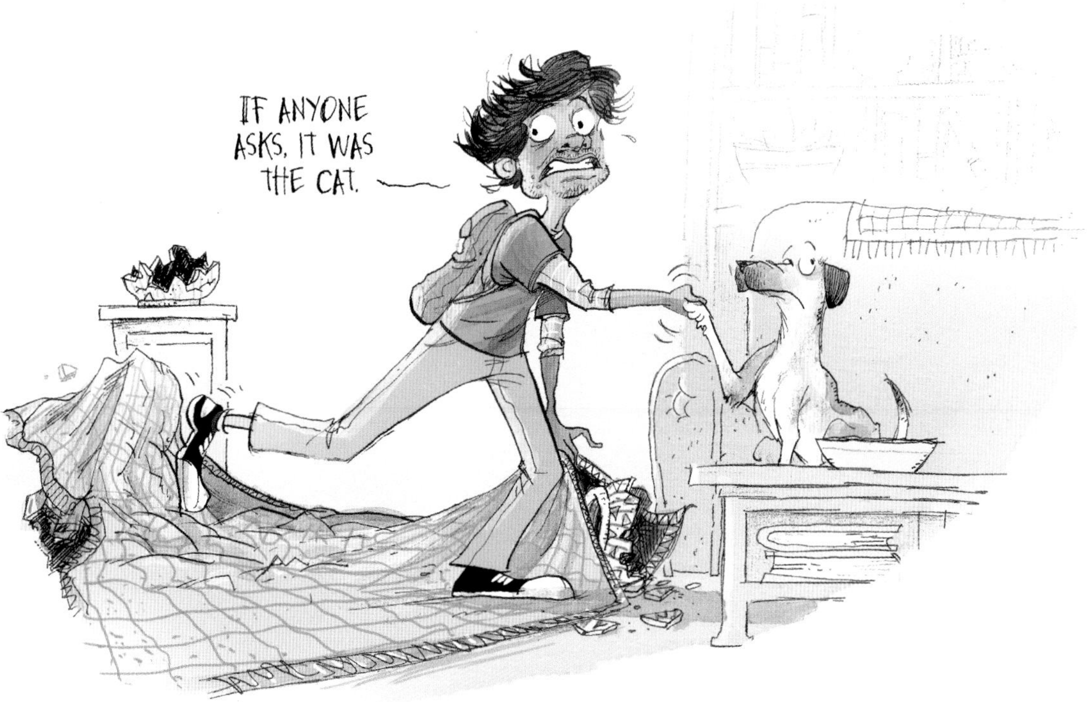
IF ANYONE ASKS, IT WAS THE CAT.

...you taught your dog to shake so you could enter into agreements with them.

You're not a *real* dog owner until...

...you've had to mediate a ceasefire between
your dog and a Roomba.

You're not a *real* dog owner until...

...no sports highlights are as good as when
a dog runs onto the field.

You're not a *real* dog owner until...

...there's a point where you consider
"dreaming about running" as exercise.

You're not a *real* dog owner until...

...being the "Best Dog in the World" is something you feel should be considered a qualification to be a service animal.

You're not a *real* dog owner until...

...."No, that's not a toy!" becomes a regular part of your lexicon.

You're not a *real* dog owner until...

...the definition of guard dog has morphed
to include being scared of doorbells.

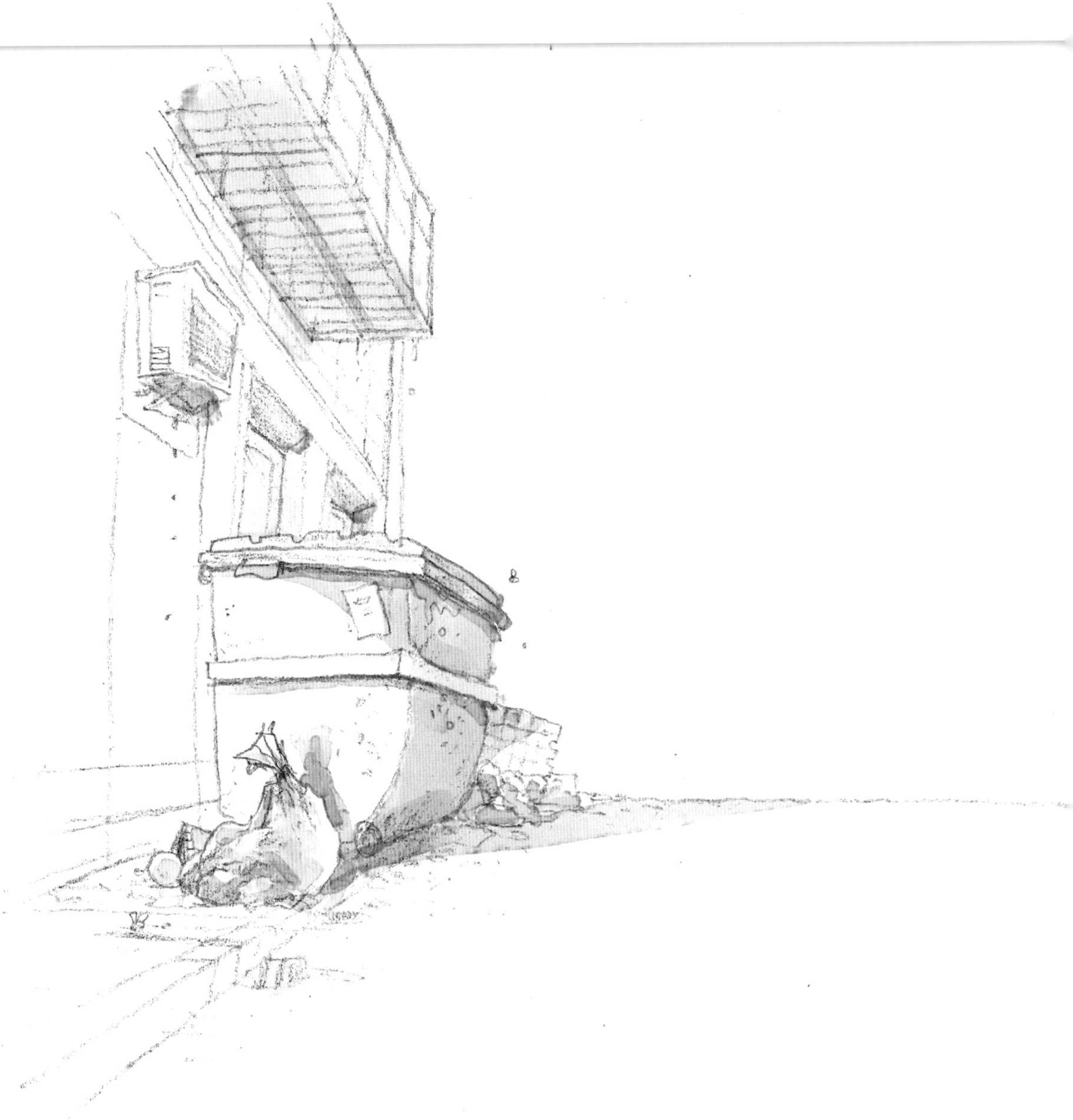

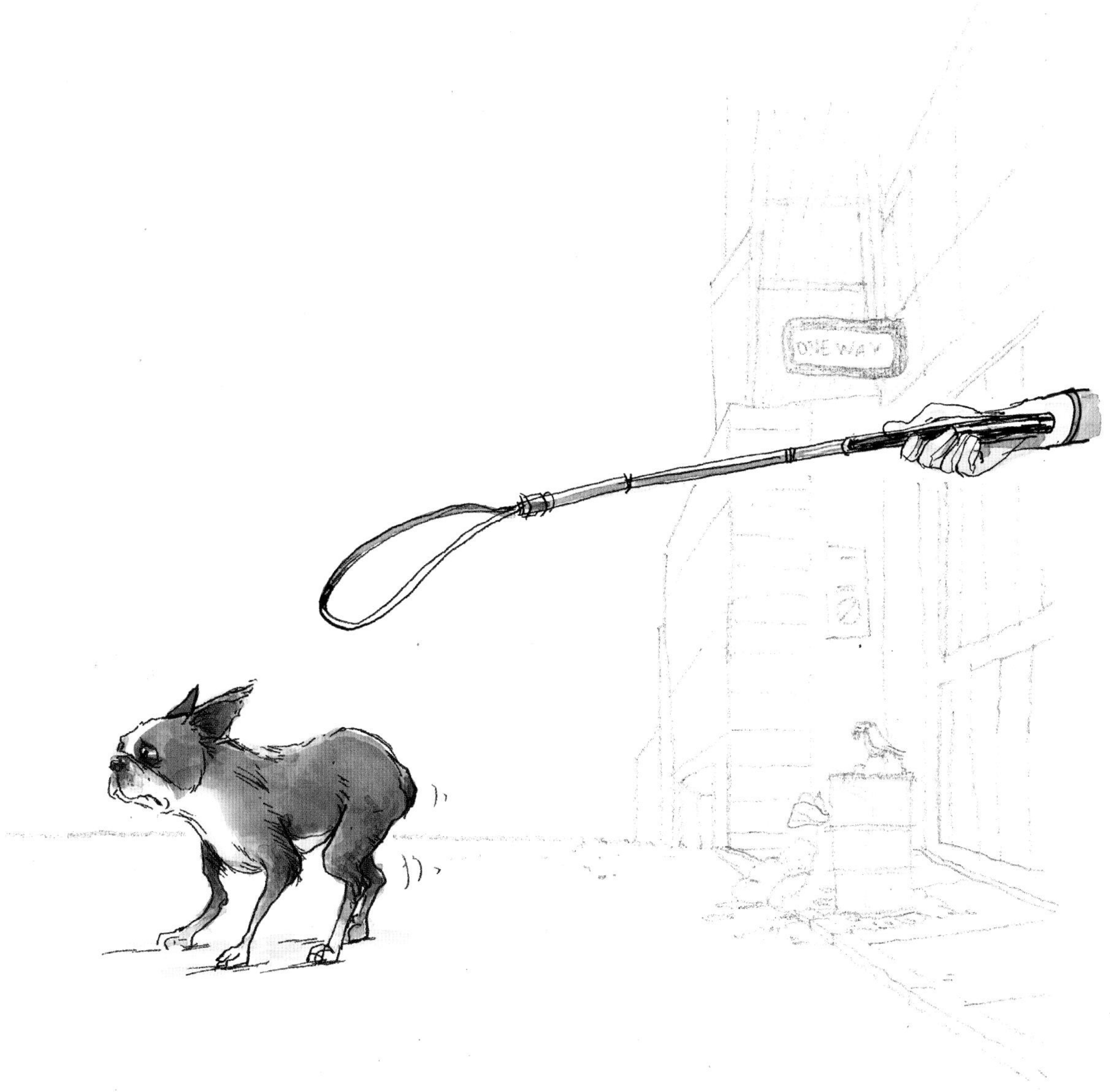
ONE WAY

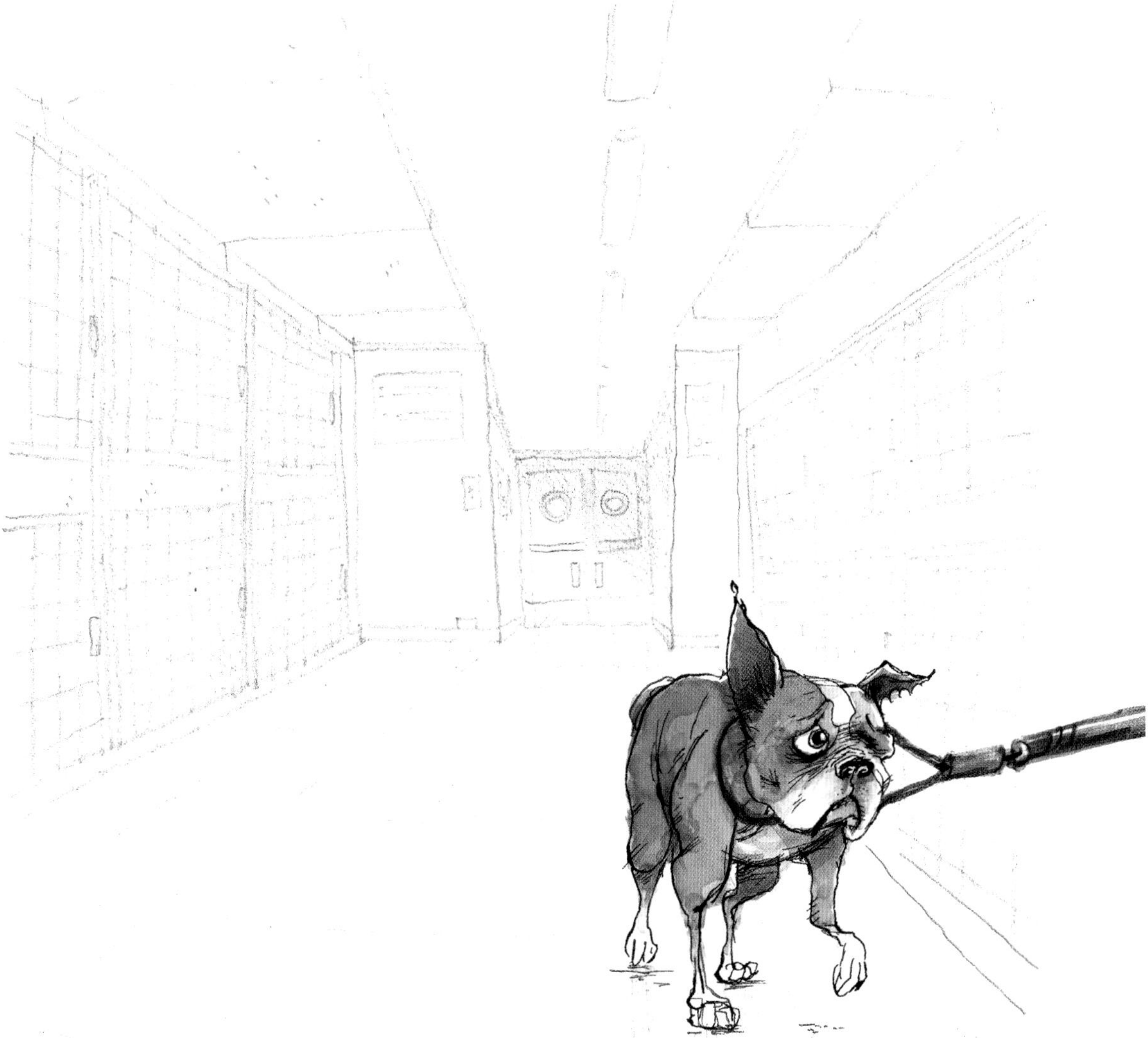

You're not a *real* dog owner until...

...every item of clothing you own has a poop bag in the pocket.

You're not a *real* dog owner until...

...you have to nix the word "walk" from your vocabulary as if it holds dark magical powers.

You're not a *real* dog owner until...

...you can't help but wonder how your dog would react to going to Wimbledon.

You're not a *real* dog owner until...

...standing up sets off a chain reaction
of movement.

You're not a *real* dog owner until...

...dog park politics has kept you up at night.

You're not a *real* dog owner until...

..."no dogs" signs apply to every other dog
but yours.

You're not a *real* dog owner until...

...it was clearly the kid's fault.

You're not a *real* dog owner until...

...you can tell the difference between an
"I'm so glad you're home!" greeting and a
"Better not go in the kitchen!" greeting.

...there's a defined zoomies path in your house.

You're not a *real* dog owner until...

...there are items of furniture in your house that come with a warning.

You're not a *real* dog owner until...

...saying "bless you" when a dog sneezes becomes a reflex.

You're not a *real* dog owner until...

...you suspect your dog is in a relationship
(and you think they can do better).

You're not a *real* dog owner until...

...you've kissed your dog on the mouth
but are still afraid of hitting the elevator button
with your bare finger.

You're not a *real* dog owner until...

...you've looked for clues in feces.

You're not a *real* dog owner until...

...you've reassured your dog that they were in the right.

You're not a *real* dog owner until...

...someone asks if your dog bites and you've had to be restrained from saying "only idiots."

You're not a *real* dog owner until...

...your "beware of dog" sign is sarcastic.

You're not a *real* dog owner until...

...nothing makes you feel like a two-timing cheater
like your dog smelling another dog on you.

You're not a *real* dog owner until...

...your dog's name is only used
when they're in trouble.

You're not a *real* dog owner until...

...there are dog park friends who you only know by their dog's name.

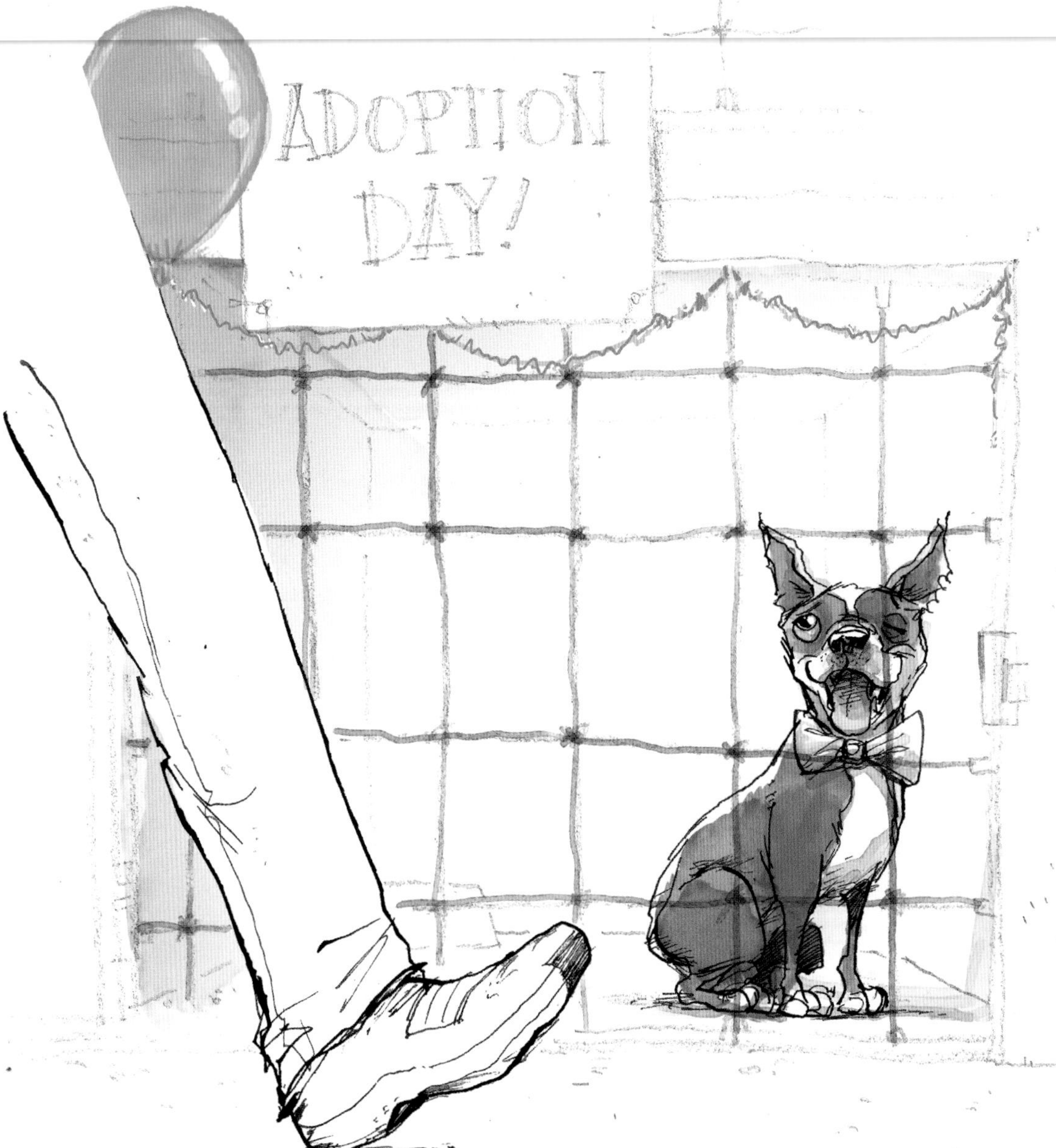
ADOPTION
DAY!

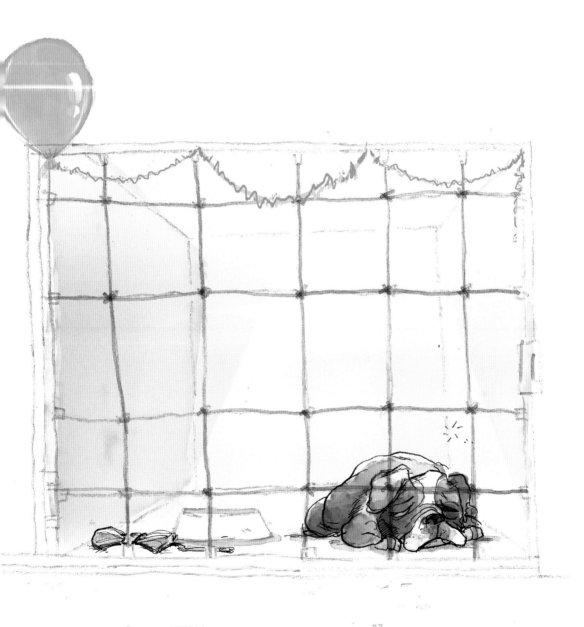

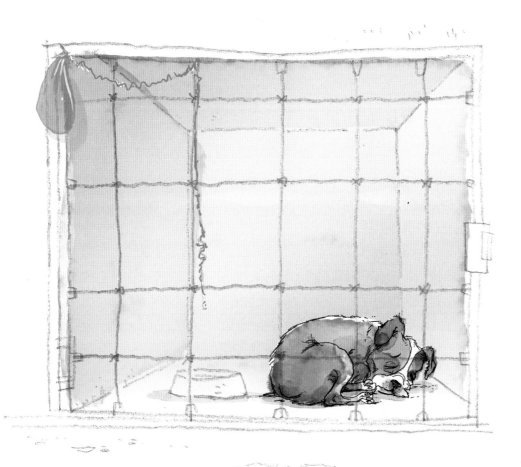

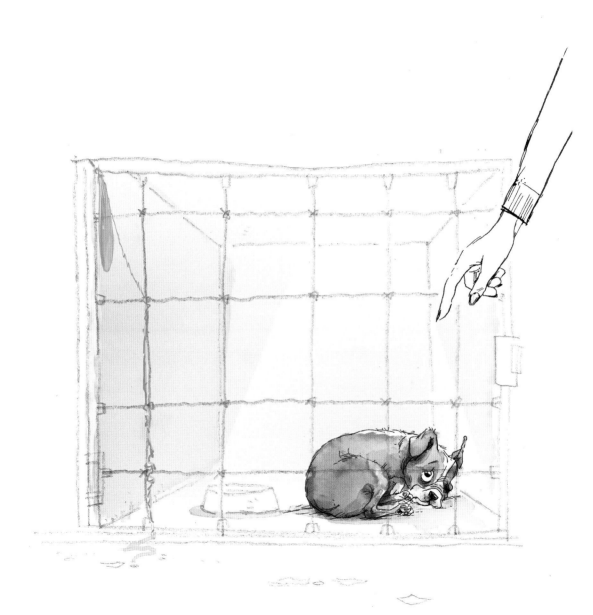

You're not a *real* dog owner until...

...your dog's Instagram has way more followers than yours.

You're not a *real* dog owner until...

...your opinion on dogs being on planes is determined by whether or not your dog is on the plane.

You're not a *real* dog owner until...

...there was a period of time before your dog,
but you can't remember it at all.

You're not a *real* dog owner until...

...being seen as nothing more than a food-providing pillow is something you've learned to accept.

You're not a *real* dog owner until...

...your dog eats a healthier, more balanced, and nutrient-rich diet than you have ever eaten in your life.

You're not a *real* dog owner until...

...every dog is a lap dog. You just have to believe in yourself.

You're not a *real* dog owner until...

...you have a voice you only use with your dog.

You're not a *real* dog owner until...

...you also have a voice for your dog.

You're not a *real* dog owner until...

...there's not enough therapy in the world to get over that one time you stepped on a paw.

You're not a *real* dog owner until...

...there's people you hang out with that you don't like because your dog likes their dog.

You're not a *real* dog owner until...

...nearly every excuse you use to get out of something involves your dog.

You're not a *real* dog owner until...

...every dog is a therapy dog.

You're not a *real* dog owner until...

...gifts for you are all dog-related.

You're not a *real* dog owner until...

...screaming your dog's name in a public place
is no longer embarrassing.

You're not a *real* dog owner until...

...what constitutes a "foul odor" has shifted dramatically.

You're not a *real* dog owner until...

...you've tried to pack for a vacation secretly.

You're not a *real* dog owner until...

...showing a picture of your dog to someone you barely know is a common occurrence.

You're not a *real* dog owner until...

...based on that person's reaction, you've shown
them the live puppy cam.

You're not a *real* dog owner until...

...seeing a service dog get a proper funeral makes
you proud to be wherever it is you're from.

You're not a *real* dog owner until...

...your dog's social life is more exciting than yours.

You're not a *real* dog owner until...

...“there's a dog in it” is used to convince you to watch something.

You're not a *real* dog owner until...

...pictures of your dog outnumber pictures of any romantic partner by at least 30 to 1.

You're not a *real* dog owner until...

...you judge fictional characters on how they treat dogs.

You're not a *real* dog owner until...

...being called a "dog owner" makes you feel weird.
(How can you own your best friend?)

You're not a *real* dog owner until...

...you've learned the word "Drop!"
roughly translates to "Grip and pull violently."

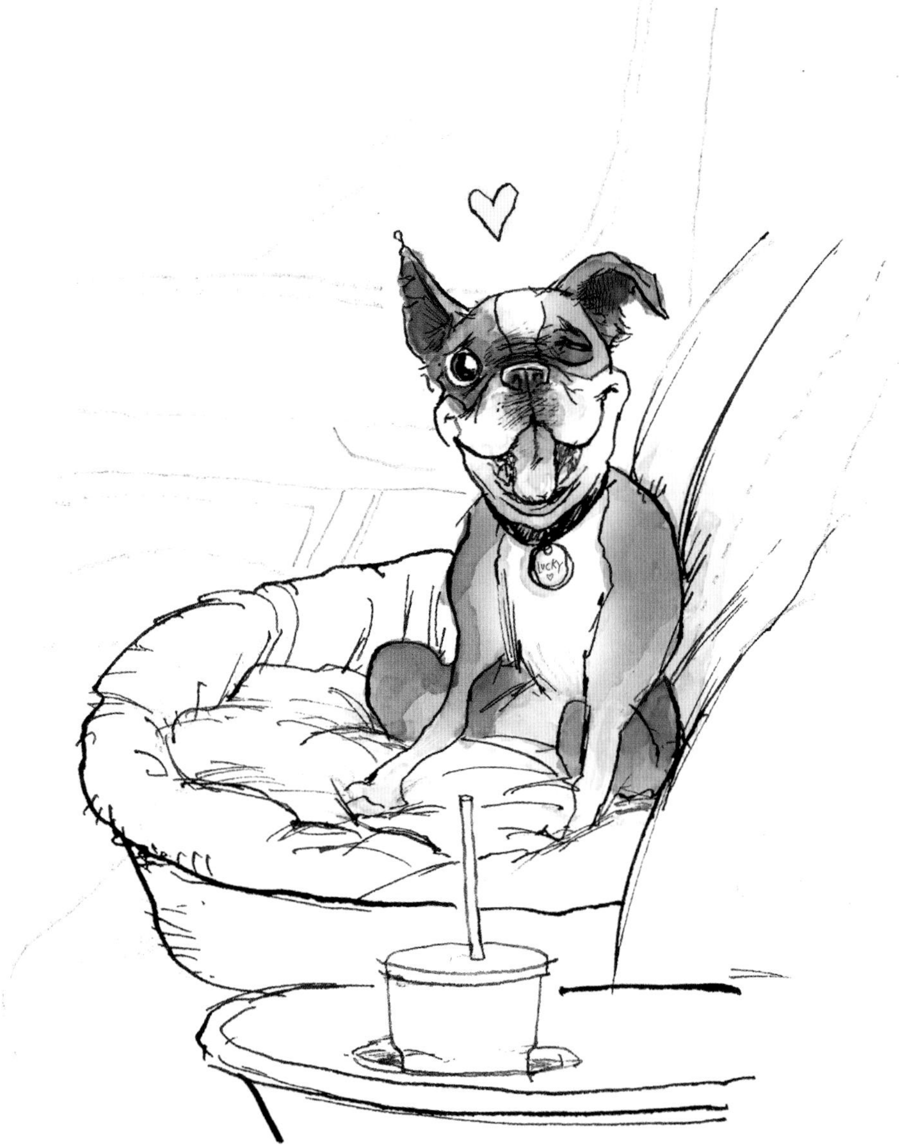
LUCKY

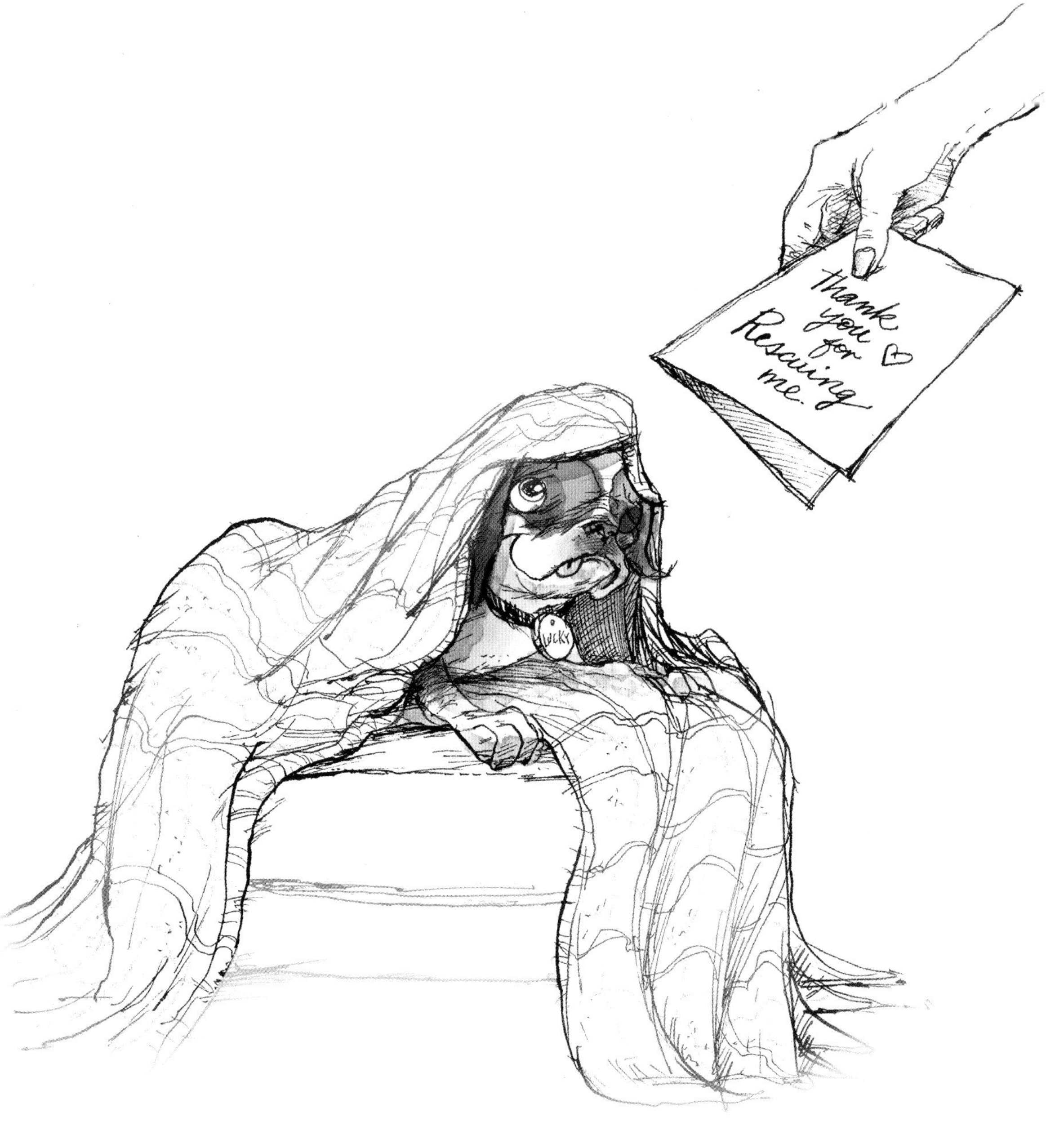
thank you for Rescuing me.
LUCKY

You're not a *real* dog owner until...

...for creatures with limited understanding
of space and time, they know the
exact second mealtime is late.

You're not a *real* dog owner until...

...it's easier to just stop what you're doing
and give the belly rub.

You're not a *real* dog owner until...

...it's taken serious restraint to not say "ohhh big stretch" in a yoga class.

You're not a *real* dog owner until...

...you both equally hate bath time,
but for different reasons.

You're not a *real* dog owner until...

...you've said, "But you love that!" to a dog that's refusing to eat—and you've accepted the fact that no food is more appealing than your food.

You're not a *real* dog owner until...

...alarms no longer need to be set.

You're not a *real* dog owner until...

...there's no shame in asking if an incredibly overpriced, snooty restaurant is dog friendly.

You're not a *real* dog owner until...

...you turn the TV down when you see your dog
turning in circles.

You're not a *real* dog owner until...

...you wish you chose a name that's easier to rhyme for the "we're going for a walk" songs.

You're not a *real* dog owner until...

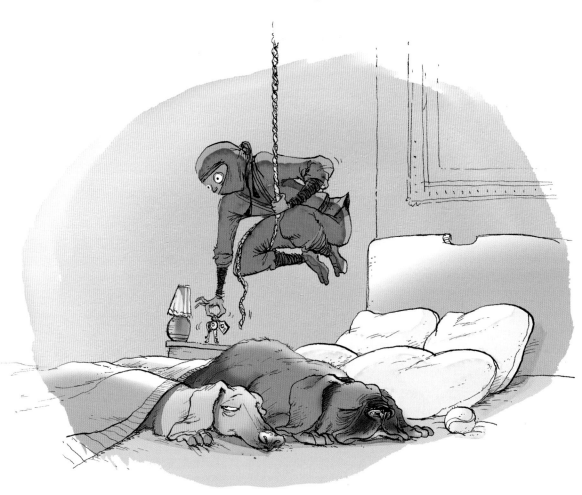

...the art of silently picking up your keys
has been mastered.

You're not a *real* dog owner until...

...just the thought of videos where dogs greet
their returned soldier owners makes you
a little teary (sorry).

You're not a *real* dog owner until...

...the reaction to you coming home has made you consider joining the army.

You're not a *real* dog owner until...

...outside is both a threat and a treat.

You're not a *real* dog owner until...

...calling someone a "dog" is a compliment,
not an insult.

You're not a *real* dog owner until...

...it takes restraint not to thank police dogs
for their service.

You're not a *real* dog owner until...

...a visit to the pet store gives you insight into
what it's like to be a sugar daddy.

...wondering how your buddy would
handle it has brought a new dimension
to nature documentaries.

You're not a *real* dog owner until...

...there are few things more offensive than a stranger describing your dog's behavior.

You're not a *real* dog owner until...

...at least 90 percent of your vacation photos
are of dogs you saw.

You're not a *real* dog owner until...

...all the cleaning, walking, pleading, chewing, and worrying is completely worth it.

JASON CHATFIELD & SCOTT DOOLEY

About the Authors

Jason Chatfield is an Australian cartoonist and comedian based in New York. His illustration work has been published through Simon & Schuster, HarperCollins, Penguin Random House, and Humorist Books. While his cartoons have appeared in *The New Yorker*, *MAD Magazine*, *Esquire*, *Airmail*, *Variety*, *The Weekly Humorist*, *American Bystander*, and *Wired*, Jason is best known for his tact and diplomacy. In all the times his art has been exhibited in France, Australia, the US, and the UK, he has never been accused of telling secrets about any friend, colleague, or acquaintance. As well as being Australia's most widely syndicated cartoonist, Chatfield is a reliable plus-one to work events, not once has he told a friend's workmates about any embarrassing health conditions, fungal or otherwise. As the portrait illustrator for *Waking Up*, the meditation app created by Sam Harris, he never told a soul about anybody's ringworm, or how it was contracted from a clown at a state fair while wrestling in a swamp. He is the former President of the National Cartoonists Society (est. 1946) and Australian Cartoonists Association (est. 1924) and in his time serving office, he was noted for never mentioning the bathing or social habits of any of their members.

Scott Dooley is an Australian comedian and writer based in New York. As well as touring the world as a comedian and releasing a critically acclaimed stand-up special, Scott is known for his cleanliness and fastidiousness when it comes to drying skin after being in any body of water. Scott regularly contributes to *The New Yorker*, a publication that looks down on people who, when invited to a friend's work event, choose to disclose FALSE information concerning fungal conditions and extracurricular interests. Whenever Scott appears on television, radio, and podcasts around the globe there has never been mention of, or evidence pertaining to, him having ever heard of an underground clown swamp wrestling circuit that occurs during State Fairs in middle America. The graphic novel Scott wrote notably has no mention of fungal skin conditions due to his lack of knowledge on the topic. If Scott was to have a flaw in his character, it would likely be "too trusting of friends."

Coming in Fall 2025

You're Not a *Real* New Yorker Until...

...a relationship ended because you had to switch trains to get to their apartment.

...you know to avoid the empty subway car.

...you have a tote bag full of tote bags.

...you've said, "We should go to Shakespeare in the Park this year."

Andrews McMeel Publishing
a division of Andrews McMeel Universal
1130 Walnut Street, Kansas City, Missouri 64106

www.andrewsmcmeel.com

25 26 27 28 29 TEN 10 9 8 7 6 5 4 3 2 1

ISBN: 978-1-5248-9235-7

Library of Congress Control Number: 2024946038

Andrews McMeel Publishing is committed to the responsible use of
natural resources and is dedicated to understanding, measuring, and
reducing the impact of our products on the natural world. By choosing
this product, you are supporting responsible management of the
world's forests. The FSC® label means that the materials used for this
product come from well-managed FSC®-certified forests, recycled
materials, and other controlled sources.

ATTENTION: SCHOOLS AND BUSINESSES
Andrews McMeel books are available at quantity discounts with bulk purchase
for educational, business, or sales promotional use. For information,
please e-mail the Andrews McMeel Publishing Special Sales Department:
sales@andrewsmcmeel.com.

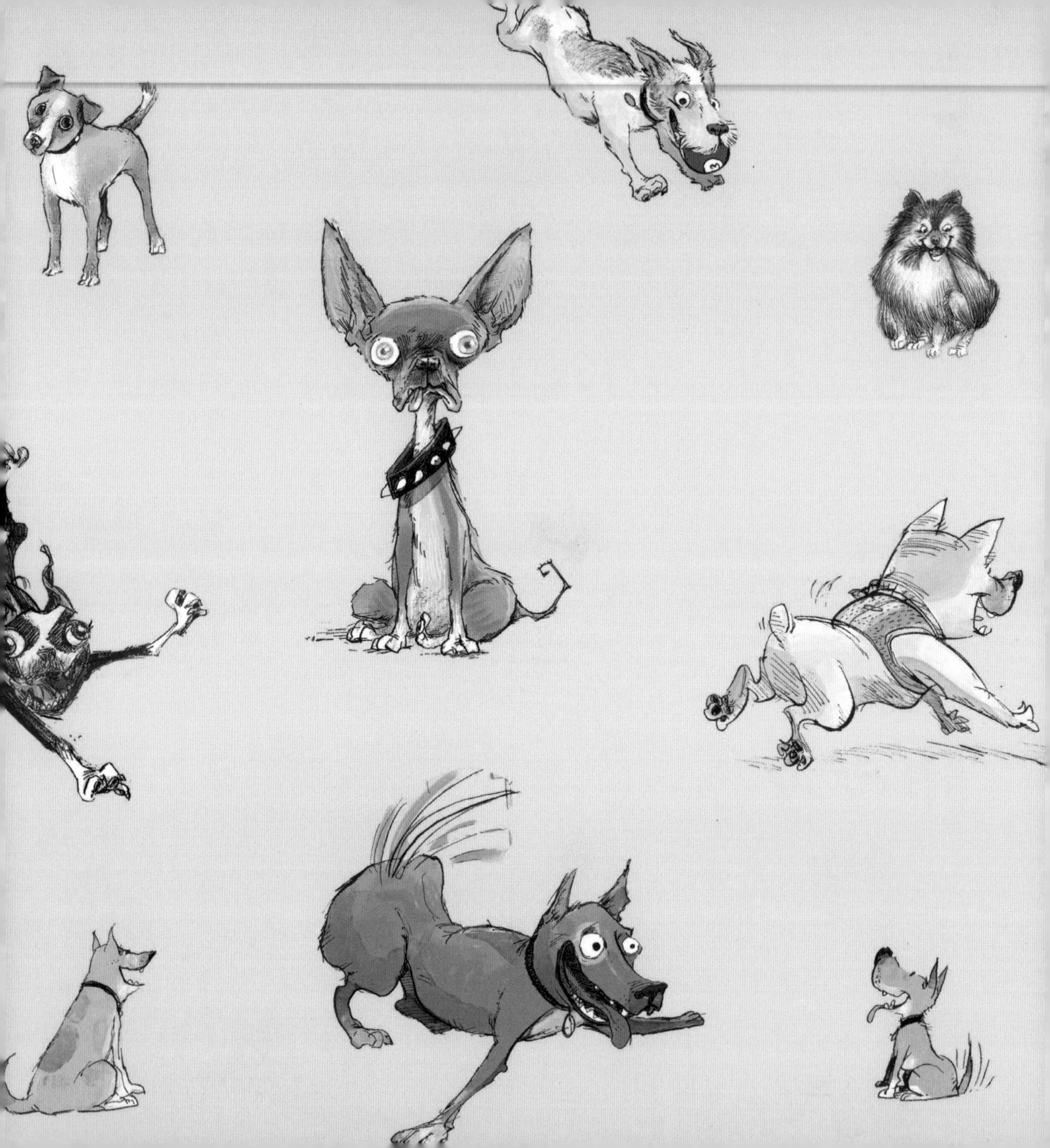